BACKYARD BIRDS

Chickadees

by Elizabeth Neuenfeldt

BLASTOFF! READERS

BELLWETHER MEDIA • MINNEAPOLIS, MN

Blastoff! Readers are carefully developed by literacy experts to build reading stamina and move students toward fluency by combining standards-based content with developmentally appropriate text.

Level 1 provides the most support through repetition of high-frequency words, light text, predictable sentence patterns, and strong visual support.

Level 2 offers early readers a bit more challenge through varied sentences, increased text load, and text-supportive special features.

Level 3 advances early-fluent readers toward fluency through increased text load, less reliance on photos, advancing concepts, longer sentences, and more complex special features.

★ **Blastoff! Universe**

Reading Level

Grade **K**

Grades **1–3**

Grade **4**

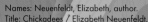

This edition first published in 2022 by Bellwether Media, Inc.

No part of this publication may be reproduced in whole or in part without written permission of the publisher. For information regarding permission, write to Bellwether Media, Inc., Attention: Permissions Department, 6012 Blue Circle Drive, Minnetonka, MN 55343.

Library of Congress Cataloging-in-Publication Data

Names: Neuenfeldt, Elizabeth, author.
Title: Chickadees / Elizabeth Neuenfeldt.
Description: Minneapolis, MN : Bellwether Media, 2022. | Series: Blastoff! readers : Backyard birds | Includes bibliographical references and index. | Audience: Ages 5-8 | Audience: Grades K-1 | Summary: "Developed by literacy experts for students in kindergarten through grade three, this book introduces chickadees to young readers through leveled text and related photos"– Provided by publisher.
Identifiers: LCCN 2021000674 (print) | LCCN 2021000675 (ebook) | ISBN 9781644874929 (library binding) | ISBN 9781648344008 (ebook)
Subjects: LCSH: Chickadees–Juvenile literature.
Classification: LCC QL696.P2615 N48 2022 (print) | LCC QL696.P2615 (ebook) | DDC 598.8/24–dc23
LC record available at https://lccn.loc.gov/2021000674
LC ebook record available at https://lccn.loc.gov/2021000675

Editor: Betsy Rathburn   Designer: Andrea Schneider

Printed in the United States of America, North Mankato, MN.

Table of Contents

What Are Chickadees?

Chickadees are small **songbirds**. They are named after the sounds they make!

There are many kinds of chickadees. Most have white, black, and gray feathers.

All in the Family

black-capped chickadee

Carolina chickadee

mountain chickadee

Life in the Trees

Chickadees live in forests. They build nests inside **cavities**.

cavity

Chickadees find food in trees. They pull **insects** from leaves and branches.

insect

Chickadees eat seeds and berries, too. They peck at seeds to open them.

Chickadee Food

insects

seeds

berries

These birds store food for winter. They hide extra seeds in **caches**.

cache

Chatty Chickadees

Chickadees live
in pairs in summer.
They live in **flocks**
in winter.

flock

pair

Chickadees make
many sounds.
One call warns
other chickadees.
Danger is near!

Chickadee Call

chickadee-
dee-
dee!

19

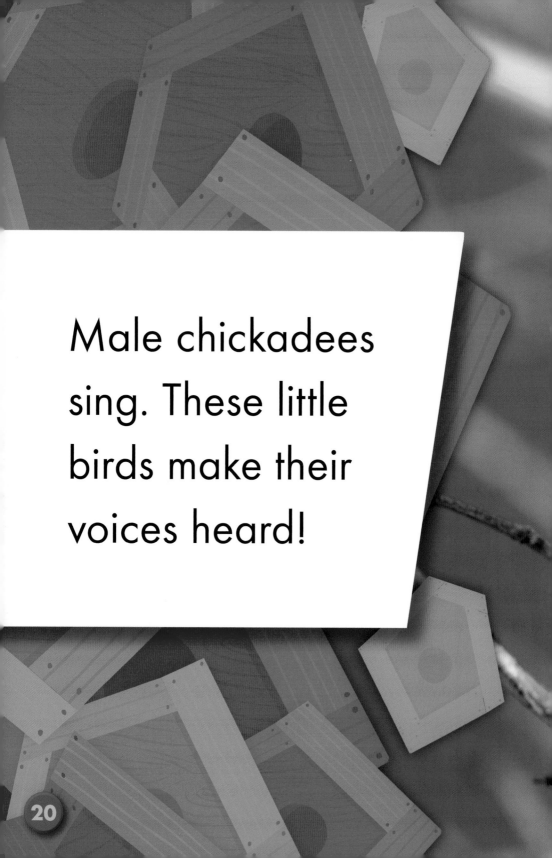

Male chickadees sing. These little birds make their voices heard!

Glossary

caches

places for hiding or storing food

insects

small animals with six legs and hard outer bodies

cavities

holes or spaces inside of things

songbirds

birds that make musical sounds

flocks

groups of birds

To Learn More

AT THE LIBRARY

Hoare, Ben. *Birds*. New York, N.Y.: DK Publishing, 2019.

Murray, Julie. *Birds*. Minneapolis, Minn.: Abdo Zoom, 2019.

Neuenfeldt, Elizabeth. *Goldfinches*. Minneapolis, Minn.: Bellwether Media, 2022.

ON THE WEB

FACTSURFER

Factsurfer.com gives you a safe, fun way to find more information.

1. Go to www.factsurfer.com.

2. Enter "chickadees" into the search box and click 🔍.

3. Select your book cover to see a list of related content.

23

Index

berries, 12
branches, 10
caches, 14, 15
call, 18, 19
cavities, 8, 9
colors, 6
family, 7
feathers, 6
flocks, 16, 17
food, 10, 13, 14
forests, 8
insects, 10, 11
kinds, 6
leaves, 10
males, 20
nests, 8

pairs, 16, 17
peck, 12
seeds, 12, 14
sing, 20
size, 4, 20
songbirds, 4
sounds, 4, 18
summer, 16
trees, 10
winter, 14, 16